Antoine and his siblings (from the left) Marie-Madeleine, Gabrielle, François, Antoine, Simone (1907)

Antoine in Le Mans, France (1921)

Antoine at Cape Juby, Morocco (1928)

Marriage to Consuelo (1931)

At Saint-Maurice I have a huge trunk. I've been filling it, ever since I was 7 years old, with my plans . . . with the letters I receive, with my photos. With all I love, think about, and want to remember. At times I spread them out haphazardly on the floor. And as I look down, I am reminded of all these things once again. Nothing but that trunk is of importance to me.

— Antoine de Saint-Exupéry

I'm not entirely sure that I've ever grown out of being a child.

— Antoine de Saint-Exupéry

Bimba Landmann has written and illustrated a number of children's books, including *I Am Marc Chagall* (Eerdmans) and *The Incredible Voyage of Ulysses* (Getty Museum). She lives in Italy. Visit her website at www.bimbalandmann.com.

© 2013 edizioni ARKA, Milano
Translation © 2014 Eerdmans Books for Young Readers
Original title: Antoine de Saint-Exupéry in cerca del piccolo principe . . .
edizioni ARKA S.r.l., Via Raffaello Sanzio 7, I-20149 Milan, Italy
www.arkaedizioni.it
www.bimbalandmann.com
www.antoinedesaintexupery.com

Published in 2014 by Eerdmans Books for Young Readers,
an imprint of Wm. B. Eerdmans Publishing Co.
2140 Oak Industrial Dr. NE
Grand Rapids, Michigan 49505
P.O. Box 163, Cambridge CB3 9PU U.K.

www.eerdmans.com/youngreaders

Manufactured at Tien Wah Press
in Malaysia in April 2014, first printing

19 18 17 16 15 14   9 8 7 6 5 4 3 2 1

Library of Congress Cataloging-in-Publication Data

Landmann, Bimba, author, illustrator.
In search of the Little Prince : the story of Antoine de Saint-Exupéry /
written and illustrated by Bimba Landmann.
pages cm
ISBN 978-0-8028-5435-3
1. Saint-Exupéry, Antoine de, 1900-1944 — Juvenile literature. 2. Authors, French — 20th
Biography — Juvenile literature. 3. Air pilots — France — Biography — Juvenile literature
PQ2637.A274Z748 2014
848'.91209 — dc23
[B]
2014004044

All quotes were originally drawn from the following Italian sources,
with English translations provided by Eerdmans Books for Young Readers:
De Saint-Exupéry, Antoine. *Opere*. Milan: Bompiani, 2000.
Guéno, Jean-Pierre. *I Ricordi del Piccolo Principe*. Milan: Bompiani, 2011.
De Saint-Exupéry, Consuelo. *Memorie della Rosa*. Siena: Lorenzo Barbera Editore S.r.l., 2007
Photos © Estate of Antoine de Saint-Exupéry-d'Aguy

FSC
www.fsc.org
MIX
Paper from
responsible sources
FSC® C012700

In Search of the Little Prince
The Story of Antoine de Saint-Exupéry

Text inspired by the works of Saint-Exupéry
Written and illustrated by

Bimba Landmann

Eerdmans Books for Young Readers
Grand Rapids, Michigan • Cambridge, U.K.

Every summer the Saint-Exupéry family descended on the chateau at Saint-Maurice:
Antoine, whom everyone called Tonio, and his four brothers and sisters.

This was the place Tonio loved most in the world.
Here he could find adventure — open a thousand doors,
explore a thousand rooms, rummage through a thousand wardrobes.
There were treasures hidden in the attic: boxes full of mystery
and trunks brimming with old clothes. The children dressed up as princes
and princesses and walked Angora rabbits as if they were exotic animals.

Those were happy days.
The evenings were happy, too, when everyone gathered in the dining room
to sing and to play the violin and piano.
Sometimes they staged fantastic stories set in faraway lands,
stories like those Tonio's mother told him as he followed her everywhere,
pulling his little green chair behind him, because he could never get
enough of them.
Oh, those faraway lands . . . those amazing names!
Tonio traced them on a map with his finger.
He dreamed of a cloud that would let him fly all over the world.

Sometimes Tonio climbed up to the top of one of the huge lime trees
surrounding the chateau.
From there he could see far off to the horizon.
"You're not afraid of anything!" his siblings shouted from below.
That wasn't true. It was just that Tonio liked to see things from above.
And he felt free up there, as free as the doves that nested among the branches.
When he reached out and lightly touched their wings,
he felt something open up inside him.
What was that feeling? Tonio couldn't describe it.
Was it a wish? A dream?
Yes — the dream of having wings that would let him fly anywhere he wanted.

Tonio loved it when night fell.
His mother would sit on the bed and smooth out the folds
in the blanket as she told him a story — ever so slowly, as he fell asleep:
"Once upon a time, a long, long time ago, there lived in a far distant land . . ."

Her words were a carpet of soft velvet that lifted Tonio high up into the sky.
The moon floated silently.
The stars drew webs of constellations: Orion . . . Andromeda . . . Pegasus . . .
Tonio closed his eyes and dreamed of a comet taking him to other worlds.

One day, the fairy tales were interrupted
by the sound of airplane engines thundering in the sky,
flying to and from a small airfield nearby.
When they whizzed just over his head, he felt something he couldn't describe.
People said the planes could fly more than three miles high!
Gazing upward, Tonio no longer dreamed of having wings,
but of actually getting into one of those flying machines.

In the meantime he tried to make his bike fly.
He created a pair of wings with planks of wood and old sheets.
But his bike didn't take off from the ground,
even though he pedaled like a madman.
He didn't become a pilot that day —
just a "first-class demon" in his aunt's eyes.

All he could do was cycle to the airfield . . .

. . . and pester the mechanics with questions:
"How does a piston work? What's an altimeter?"

"Would you like to fly, son?" a pilot asked him one day.
"I . . . yes, yes, sir. I'd love to very much . . ." Tonio stammered.
"How old are you?"
"Twelve, sir." The truth.
"Has your mother given you permission?"
"Yes!" said Tonio. A lie.
A lie that let him fly higher than the doves, higher than the clouds.

What a feeling! But who could he tell? Certainly not his mother!
He rushed home and, inspired, wrote:
"The wings quivered in the evening breeze.
The engine's song lulled the sleeping soul.
The sun brushed us with its pale color."
Only twelve years old, Tonio had fallen in love with flying and with poetry.

But the excitement he felt that summer didn't last. Soon after, war broke out,
and Tonio could no longer go wandering around the airfield.
Now military planes flew overhead.
The roar of engines signaled bombs and destruction.

And yet, Tonio was still fascinated by airplanes.
From Paris, where he was studying, he wrote to his mother:
"The whole sky trembles . . . it feels like being in the middle of a full-scale
hurricane, of a storm at sea. It's wonderful."
Tonio was eighteen years old, and war was just an adventure to him.

He was drafted into an aviation regiment as a mechanic.
But that wasn't what he wanted! He wanted to *fly* planes,
even if he had to borrow money from his mother to pay for flying lessons.
The desire to fly was irresistible. Perhaps, he felt, it was his destiny:
"If I fail, I'll be very sad — but I'll succeed," he wrote to his mother,
filling his letters with pictures of airplanes.

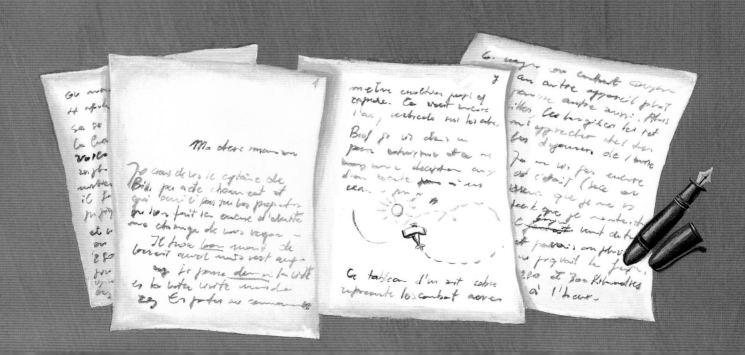

His mother tried to talk him out of it:
"Tonio, flying airplanes is so dangerous! Don't you know how many planes crash?"
But stopping him would be like clipping a butterfly's wings.
She gave in.
And Tonio finally learned to fly planes.
Finally he was as free as the doves.
When he was told he would be leaving for Morocco, he was thrilled:
"The desert must look beautiful from a plane."

In Morocco, however, there were no long missions in the desert.
He spent most of his time doing drills above Casablanca and the airport barracks.
Sometimes, even though he shouldn't have, he ventured further.
He longed to fly higher and higher.
Miles in the air, he found perfect calm and solitude.
Then at night, by the flickering lamplight, he read, drew, and wrote letters.

He also wrote poetry.
Because writing had begun to make him fly, too.
It had wings that could carry him far away.

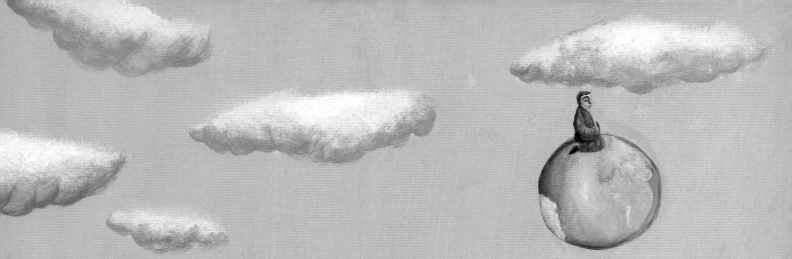

When he returned to France, Tonio finally got his pilot's license.
He couldn't wait to fly!
So one day he hopped into a plane without permission.
But the plane crashed, and Tonio broke his skull.
That was the end of military planes for him!
He had to stop, find a job, leave the freedom of the skies.
He found work as an accountant, but it made Tonio feel like
a swallow locked in a cage.
He spent his time watching the hands of the clock tick.
He wrote to a friend:
"It's exactly ten minutes past eleven.
It's exactly eleven minutes past eleven.
It's exactly twelve minutes past eleven."

Only writing gave him comfort.
Short stories. Stories to calm his desire to flee.
And to try and get his soul, heavier and heavier by the day, to fly.
"What's wrong with you?" his friends asked him. "You've got a
good job; you earn plenty. What more do you want?"

Tonio's coworkers only ever talked about money, houses, golf, and cars.
They did not feel, as he did, that they were the inhabitants of a
wandering planet suspended in the Milky Way.
"I'm bored," he sighed.
He needed to be in touch with the wind, with the stars.
He had to start flying again.

Then fate smiled on Tonio.
Mail was starting to be delivered to other continents by planes,
and there was soon a huge demand for pilots.
Tonio started flying again, carrying letters between France and Africa.
He even became manager of a stopover in Morocco, in the middle of the desert.
Every week planes from France would land there to refuel.
Inside the hold of each plane were thousands of precious letters,
words entrusted to him so they might get to their destination,
despite the thousands of obstacles in the desert —
sandstorms, breakdowns, uneasy meetings with Bedouins.

When there were no flights to schedule,
Tonio established contacts with the tribes of the desert.
The stopover was in their territory, and it was important to be friends with them.
It was easy to make friends with the children. They were not afraid
to approach this white man who always had chocolate in his pockets!
With the adults, though, he needed to be more patient — to overcome their
distrust, learn Arabic, show them the flying machines, invite them to tea.
They gradually allowed themselves to be won over by this "commander of birds,"
as they so kindly called him.

He was also taming a desert fox:
"It's as wild as a beast and roars like a lion,"
he wrote to his mother.

Tonio lived close to his little fox, and it wasn't long before it was his turn
to be tamed by the desert.
He listened to the silence.
He listened to the night's whispers.
He listened to the infinite space in which the earth floats.
And amid the vast expanse of sand and under the vast expanse of stars,
he felt free.

Then he walked back into his hut,
full of the silence he had just been listening to.
It wasn't an empty silence, but one that was waiting for what comes next.
A blank page on which to start writing.

In that remote corner of Africa, in the silence of the desert,
in his bare hut, Tonio started writing a novel.
He jotted down his thoughts and his emotions.
He wrote about the desert, about the various tribes.
He wrote about his life as a pilot, and also about what he missed from his childhood.
He wrote as lightly as if he were flying —
and for Tonio, writing was like flying,
like visiting the places of his soul and the landscapes of his emotions.
He titled his novel *Southern Mail*.

Back in Paris, Tonio started looking for a publisher who might be interested
in publishing his novel. Once again fate smiled on him.
Now he wasn't just a pilot. He was also an author: Antoine de Saint-Exupéry.
The publisher was so excited that he immediately asked Antoine to write seven
more novels!
Antoine was excited, too, but he wanted to go find other adventures,
more wonders to write about.
So he took a new job as director of the postal service in Argentina.
With just enough time to pack a couple of suits and shoes,
Antoine was off again — as light as a bird.

In Argentina, Antoine explored new routes and made plenty of money.
But he was not happy. He was almost thirty. What was missing?
Perhaps a rose to love?
Yes — a rose named Consuelo.
They met one evening at a friend's house in Buenos Aires.
Antoine instantly fell in love with Consuelo, and that very evening
he took her for a plane ride over the city, to show her the stars, to talk about his
wanderer's soul, to offer her everything, immediately: his heart, his name, his life.

Consuelo was charmed by this poet, this flying knight
who spoke magic words, who wrote her letters that were forty,
a hundred pages long.
Antoine and Consuelo married in France.

Soon after, his novel became a best seller.
It was even made into a film!
The phone in the Saint-Exupéry household never stopped ringing.
Antoine had a busy schedule: dinners, parties, and meetings.
He went to cafés, told stories, made other people laugh with his card tricks.
He spent lots of money.
He played the joker.
He laughed.
He laughed, but there was a strange sadness in his eyes.
Maybe he was missing the silence of the desert?
Or perhaps the freedom of flying away in search of something new?

"I prefer night storms to the conversations one hears in Parisian cafés;
my planes are the only things that can save me," he wrote.

Antoine began flying again.
He never complained about the gusts of rain, the storms and lightning,
the frost at night, and the dark dragons when he was afraid.
He didn't complain, even when he crashed his plane and broke his bones.
Once, twice, three times, and more.
"I'm happy with my job; I feel I'm a farmer of the stars," he said every time.

Flying planes and writing were all that mattered to him.
He flew over Paris, Casablanca, Buenos Aires, New York.
He wrote *Night Flight* and *Wind, Sand, and Stars*.
Every day a different hotel room.
His life was a flight.
It was in flight.

And yet one day everything came to a halt.
War had driven the world mad again.
Antoine wanted to enlist and serve France, his country,
but he was told that he was too old for reconnaissance flights.
"War is not an adventure. War is like a disease," he said sadly.
He would love to help the world heal.
Instead he felt powerless. He could do nothing.

On the 25th floor of his concrete building in New York,
he had never felt so alone.
He had just one wish — to be allowed to fly again.
To fly like the small paper airplanes he threw from the window.
Sometimes they glided softly, and sometimes they twisted in the air.
Once one fell on a policeman's head,
and he came up to Antoine's apartment to tell him off!

As he waited, Antoine wrote letters.
Every once in a while, on a blank sheet, he drew the outline of a child.
Perhaps it was a young poet. Perhaps it was the prince of some unknown planet . . .
he didn't know yet. But the boy kept him company, and Antoine liked drawing him.
The child began to visit him more and more often.

"Turn him into the main character of a fairy tale!" his publisher suggested.
Really? Tell a fairy tale during wartime?
Wouldn't it be better to write a book that would make people think?

His pen, however, continued to draw the boy.
Golden hair.
Frail body.
Two dots for eyes, like two stars.
Where was he from? Maybe from a wandering planet suspended in the Milky Way?
Where did Antoine meet him?
In the desert? Like the one where his airplane once broke down?

The more Antoine drew, the more the boy resembled him.
Like him, the boy didn't understand people who want to be rich.
He too was sad at seeing his planet smothered by baobabs,
the way the earth was smothered by war.
He too had tamed a fox.
He too loved a rose . . .

Antoine wrote a fairy tale like the ones he used to listen to as a child:
it was a fairy tale about a little prince who came from far away,
and it helped him find the innocence of his childhood once more,
when he was simply Tonio.

He wrote the story a few months before he set off on his last mission.

Antoine was called back to France, to fly again.
Everyone's help was needed to put an end to this crazy war.
Antoine had to fly between Sardinia and Corsica.
His missions were dangerous. The sky was full of enemy planes.
But, strangely, he was not afraid of dying.
Maybe he imagined himself ending up on a star.

One morning, on the 31st of July 1944, he set off from Corsica.
By that afternoon, there was no trace of Antoine.
His plane seemed to have vanished into thin air.
Antoine had vanished into thin air.
He was just 44 years old.

The Little Prince survived him — and survived those crazy times.
It has survived all the time and space and history between then and now.
It has been translated into two hundred fifty languages, and read by millions of people.

What is it that makes this story so beloved?
Maybe its secret is something like the one the fox reveals to the little prince:
"It is only with the heart that one can see rightly.
What is essential is invisible to the eye."

One morning you wake up and say:
"It was just a fairy tale."
You laugh at yourself, but deep down you're not laughing at all.
You know that fairy tales are the only truth of life.

— Antoine de Saint-Exupéry